Ivy
and the
Hummingbird

Written by
Janice McMorris

Illustrated by
Estelle Corke

Published by Miriam Laundry Publishing Company
miriamlaundry.com

Caldwell, Idaho.
Library of Congress Control Number: 2023907934

HC ISBN 978-1-998816-54-5
PB ISBN 978-1-998816-47-7
e-Book ISBN 978-1-998816-48-4

FIRST EDITION

To Reagan, Clark and Maggie,
with love.

Inspired by my mom,
who taught me about hummingbirds.

Ivy was very brave. She used to be afraid of loud noises, but then things changed.

She used to be afraid of the loud mooing of the huge cows in the pasture next door. That was until one morning when a cow stuck its head in her window. "Moo! Moo!" it bellowed, waking her up. Ivy's eyes opened wide.

"Moo! Moo!"

She shouted, "Shoo! Shoo!" Ivy watched, laughing, as the cow hurried back to the pasture where it belonged.

Ivy used to be afraid of owls hooting and frogs croaking at night. That was until her little sister, Molly, and her cousin, Carl, started a game on the front porch. "Hoot! Hoot! Croak! Croak!" They all hooted, croaked, and laughed under the night sky.

"Hoot! Hoot!"

6

7

Then Mama said, "It's time for all little owls and frogs to go to bed."

So, they all hopped and flew to their beds. Even Mama!

"Boom!"

Ivy used to be afraid of thunderstorms. That was until she huddled on the couch with Molly and Carl under a snuggly blanket, while the thunder clapped and the wind howled. "Boom!" roared the thunder. "Whoosh!" whistled the wind.

10

"Whoosh!"

Together with her family,
Ivy felt safe in the storm.

11

But one day, Ivy heard a new noise, and it was VERY scary!

On the morning of the new VERY scary noise, Ivy walked through the garden and said, "Good morning, kitty cat. Good morning, dogs. Good morning, butterflies. Good morning, ladybugs."

Ivy loved the garden. She checked on the berries and the grapes.

She was about to pick some ripe,
red strawberries

when suddenly...

A loud, startling noise buzzed right past her head! "WHAT WAS THAT?!" Ivy shrieked.

She ran into the house and peered out the window. Ivy waited and watched, but she didn't see anything.

"Bzzzzzzzzzzzzzzzzzzz

zzzz!"

17

Ivy was curious. She quietly tiptoed out the door
to look for the terrible buzzing thing.

As she moved closer to the flower garden,
she heard it again.

"Bzzzzz!"

She felt the whir of wings, but it was so fast, she couldn't see what it was. Ivy ran back inside.

"My goodness, Ivy!" Grandma exclaimed.
"What's wrong?"

"Get back, Grandma!" shouted Ivy. "There
is a terrible buzzing thing out there!"

Ivy and Grandma peered through the window. Ivy was still curious.

"Grandma, will ... will you come outside with me and see what it is?"

Ivy and Grandma walked cautiously toward the garden together.

Grandma stopped and smiled. "Hello hummingbird," she said.

She told Ivy to stand very still. Ivy didn't move or make a sound.

The hummingbird hovered right in front of Ivy, as if to say hello!

Then the hummingbird darted away to drink nectar from a petunia. It chirped and fluttered from petunia to fuchsia to cardinal flower.

As Ivy watched, another hummingbird darted past, and the two birds flew into the air doing flips and even flew backward! Ivy couldn't believe her eyes! She laughed in delight.

The hummingbirds' wings beat so fast they were nearly invisible. But when the tiny birds landed on a tree branch, Ivy saw that they were barely bigger than her thumb. They were a shiny greenish color and had long beaks.

"Oh Grandma! How could I have been afraid of such a tiny little bird?" Ivy laughed again.

"Hummingbirds are very special to me," Grandma told Ivy. "My mother taught me about them long ago when I was your age."

Ivy watched as the hummingbirds darted away, hovered, and then flew back. And every day after, Ivy spent time in the garden, waiting and watching. Sometimes Molly and Carl watched with her.

She watched the hummingbirds until the winter came and they migrated to warmer places.

When spring finally arrived, Ivy made sure to water the flowers, so the hummingbirds had nectar to drink when they returned.

She smiled and remembered that sometimes, if she was very still and quiet, a hummingbird would hover close to her, as if to say hello.